# SUPER HERO
## MAD LIBS®

concept created by **Roger Price & Leonard Stern**

Mad Libs
An Imprint of Penguin Random House

MAD LIBS
Penguin Young Readers Group
An Imprint of Penguin Random House LLC

Concept created by Roger Price & Leonard Stern

Published by Mad Libs,
an imprint of Penguin Random House LLC,
345 Hudson Street, New York, New York 10014.
Printed in the USA.

ISBN 9780843182712

9 10

# MAD LIBS
# INSTRUCTIONS

MAD LIBS® is a game for people who don't like games! It can be played by one, two, three, four, or forty.

## • RIDICULOUSLY SIMPLE DIRECTIONS

In this tablet you will find stories containing blank spaces where words are left out. One player, the READER, selects one of these stories. The READER does not tell anyone what the story is about. Instead, he/she asks the other players, the WRITERS, to give him/her words. These words are used to fill in the blank spaces in the story.

## • TO PLAY

The READER asks each WRITER in turn to call out a word—an adjective or a noun or whatever the space calls for—and uses them to fill in the blank spaces in the story. The result is a MAD LIBS® game.

When the READER then reads the completed MAD LIBS® game to the other players, they will discover that they have written a story that is fantastic, screamingly funny, shocking, silly, crazy, or just plain dumb—depending upon which words each WRITER called out.

## • EXAMPLE (*Before* and *After*)

" _____ !" he said _____
                EXCLAMATION                                    ADVERB

as he jumped into his convertible _____ and
                                                    NOUN

drove off with his _____ wife.
                              ADJECTIVE

" _____*Ouch*_____ !" he said _____*stupidly*_____
                EXCLAMATION                                    ADVERB

as he jumped into his convertible _____*cat*_____ and
                                                    NOUN

drove off with his _____*brave*_____ wife.
                              ADJECTIVE

In case you have forgotten what adjectives, adverbs, nouns, and verbs are, here is a quick review:

An ADJECTIVE describes something or somebody. *Lumpy, soft, ugly, messy,* and *short* are adjectives.

An ADVERB tells how something is done. It modifies a verb and usually ends in "ly." *Modestly, stupidly, greedily,* and *carefully* are adverbs.

A NOUN is the name of a person, place, or thing. *Sidewalk, umbrella, bridle, bathtub,* and *nose* are nouns.

A VERB is an action word. *Run, pitch, jump,* and *swim* are verbs. Put the verbs in past tense if the directions say PAST TENSE. *Ran, pitched, jumped,* and *swam* are verbs in the past tense.

When we ask for A PLACE, we mean any sort of place: a country or city (*Spain, Cleveland*) or a room (*bathroom, kitchen*).

An EXCLAMATION or SILLY WORD is any sort of funny sound, gasp, grunt, or outcry, like *Wow!, Ouch!, Whomp!, Ick!,* and *Gadzooks!*

When we ask for specific words, like a NUMBER, a COLOR, an ANIMAL, or a PART OF THE BODY, we mean a word that is one of those things, like *seven, blue, horse,* or *head*.

When we ask for a PLURAL, it means more than one. For example, *cat* pluralized is *cats*.

MAD LIBS® is fun to play with friends, but you can also play it by yourself! To begin with, DO NOT look at the story on the page below. Fill in the blanks on this page with the words called for. Then, using the words you have selected, fill in the blank spaces in the story.

Now you've created your own hilarious MAD LIBS® game!

# THE MAN OF STEEL

ADJECTIVE _____

VERB _____

VERB ENDING IN "ING" _____

PART OF THE BODY _____

ADVERB _____

VERB ENDING IN "ING" _____

COLOR _____

ADJECTIVE _____

NOUN _____

ADVERB _____

NOUN _____

NOUN _____

NOUN _____

# MAD LIBS

# THE MAN OF STEEL

**DC COMICS™**

Special report to the *Daily Planet* by Lois Lane: The _____
_____ADJECTIVE_____

quiet of the afternoon was broken by a/an _____ for help after
_____VERB_____

the safety harness of a construction worker _____ on
_____VERB ENDING IN "ING"_____

the eighty-seventh floor of the Metropolis Tower malfunctioned. The

man held on to the building's scaffolding with one _____
_____PART OF THE BODY_____

while his friends tried to save him. Before they could reach him, the

man lost his grip and began to fall _____ toward the ground
_____ADVERB_____

. . . when suddenly a blue-and-red figure came _____
_____VERB ENDING IN "ING"_____

down from out of the clear _____ sky toward the tower! "It's
_____COLOR_____

going to be _____?" a woman cried. The Man of _____
_____ADJECTIVE_____            _____NOUN_____

swooped in to save the falling man, as _____ as a/an
_____ADVERB_____

_____. On the street, the people gave a cheer for the
_____NOUN_____

_____ of Metropolis, who had once again saved the
_____NOUN_____

_____!
_____NOUN_____

From DC COMICS SUPER HERO MAD LIBS® • TM & © DC Comics. (s15).
Published in 2015 by Mad Libs, an imprint of Penguin Random House LLC.

MAD LIBS® is fun to play with friends, but you can also play it by yourself! To begin with, DO NOT look at the story on the page below. Fill in the blanks on this page with the words called for. Then, using the words you have selected, fill in the blank spaces in the story.

Now you've created your own hilarious MAD LIBS® game!

# HOT AND COLD

ADJECTIVE _____

NOUN _____

PERSON IN ROOM _____

NOUN _____

VERB _____

NOUN _____

ADJECTIVE _____

PLURAL NOUN _____

NUMBER _____

COLOR _____

ADJECTIVE _____

NOUN _____

ADJECTIVE _____

ADJECTIVE _____

PLURAL NOUN _____

PART OF THE BODY _____

PLURAL NOUN _____

A PLACE _____

# MAD LIBS

# HOT AND COLD

As an alarm began to sound, The Flash flew at _____ speed to
                                             ADJECTIVE

discover his _____, Captain Cold, running away from
              NOUN

_____'s Jewelry Store. But just as the Fastest _____
PERSON IN ROOM                                              NOUN

Alive was about to subdue Captain Cold, another alarm started to

_____! This time, it was caused by Heat Wave, who was
VERB

robbing a/an _____ across the street! *This calls for some*
              NOUN

_____ *thinking!* The Flash said to himself. He thought a
ADJECTIVE

moment and then started to run back and forth between the two

_____ so fast, it looked like there were _____ Flashes!
PLURAL NOUN                                         NUMBER

Both villains believed the _____ Speedster was coming for
                            COLOR

them and fired their _____ weapons at him! But when the
                      ADJECTIVE

_____ of Heat Wave's heat weapon hit the cold from Captain
NOUN

Cold's _____ weapon, it turned into a/an _____
        ADJECTIVE                                  ADJECTIVE

cloud of _____. Faster than the _____ could see,
          PLURAL NOUN                     PART OF THE BODY

The Flash disarmed the _____ just as the police arrived to
                        PLURAL NOUN

cart the criminals away to (the) _____.
                                  A PLACE

From DC COMICS SUPER HERO MAD LIBS® • TM & © DC Comics. (s15).
Published in 2015 by Mad Libs, an imprint of Penguin Random House LLC.

MAD LIBS® is fun to play with friends, but you can also play it by yourself! To begin with, DO NOT look at the story on the page below. Fill in the blanks on this page with the words called for. Then, using the words you have selected, fill in the blank spaces in the story.

Now you've created your own hilarious MAD LIBS® game!

# CHEETAHS NEVER PROSPER

ADJECTIVE _____

ANIMAL _____

A PLACE _____

ADJECTIVE _____

NOUN _____

ADJECTIVE _____

EXCLAMATION _____

NOUN _____

ANIMAL _____

VERB ENDING IN "ING" _____

ADJECTIVE _____

COLOR _____

ADJECTIVE _____

ADJECTIVE _____

NOUN _____

ANIMAL _____

A/An _____ crowd gathered at the City Zoo to view the rare
ADJECTIVE

jeweled _____ of (the) _____ statue that was on
ANIMAL                           A PLACE

display. Wonder Woman was also in attendance, and her job was to

guard the _____ statue. *This is just the sort of* _____
ADJECTIVE                                                        NOUN

*that would interest the Cheetah,* she thought. Suddenly, a/an

_____ roar sounded out. "_____!" the Amazon
ADJECTIVE                           EXCLAMATION

_____ cried. She ran outside to see a/an _____ that
NOUN                                                ANIMAL

had escaped from its enclosure _____ at a group of
                                VERB ENDING IN "ING"

_____ children. Wonder Woman quickly flung her
ADJECTIVE

_____ lasso to tame the _____ beast . . . while inside,
COLOR                            ADJECTIVE

the Cheetah laughed as she pushed her way through the crowd and

grabbed the _____ statue. "While Wonder Woman plays the
ADJECTIVE

_____, I'll make this little pretty my own!" But when the
NOUN

Cheetah tried to escape with her loot, she found her way blocked by a

snarling _____ at the end of a golden leash . . . held by none
ANIMAL

other than Wonder Woman!

MAD LIBS® is fun to play with friends, but you can also play it by yourself! To begin with, DO NOT look at the story on the page below. Fill in the blanks on this page with the words called for. Then, using the words you have selected, fill in the blank spaces in the story.

Now you've created your own hilarious MAD LIBS® game!

# GREEN LANTERN'S LIGHT

NOUN _____

ADJECTIVE _____

NOUN _____

COLOR _____

VERB _____

A PLACE _____

PART OF THE BODY _____

PLURAL NOUN _____

FIRST NAME (MALE) _____

A PLACE _____

ADJECTIVE _____

OCCUPATION _____

ADJECTIVE _____

ADJECTIVE _____

NOUN _____

NOUN _____

ADJECTIVE _____

# MAD LIBS®
# GREEN LANTERN'S LIGHT

After Green Lantern easily put out a raging _____ in a
<br>NOUN

warehouse, a/an _____ firefighter asked him, "Man, where
<br>ADJECTIVE

can I get a power _____ like yours?" _____ Lantern
<br>NOUN      COLOR

responded, "This ring allows its wearer to _____ anything
<br>VERB

they can imagine, and it was created by the Guardians of (the)

_____. It's meant to be worn by _____-selected
<br>A PLACE                          PART OF THE BODY

peace officers from _____ across the universe. I received
<br>PLURAL NOUN

mine from _____ when his spaceship crashed here on
<br>FIRST NAME (MALE)

(the) _____. He was injured in the _____ accident
<br>A PLACE                          ADJECTIVE

and had to find someone to pass the ring on to. I was a test

_____ at an aircraft company when the ring found me and
<br>OCCUPATION

made me into a/an _____ hero. But only the _____
<br>ADJECTIVE                          ADJECTIVE

can wear the _____ and be a Green _____ . . . just
<br>NOUN                          NOUN

like it takes a/an _____ person to be a firefighter like you!"
<br>ADJECTIVE

From DC COMICS SUPER HERO MAD LIBS® • TM & © DC Comics. (s15).
Published in 2015 by Mad Libs, an imprint of Penguin Random House LLC.

MAD LIBS® is fun to play with friends, but you can also play it by yourself! To begin with, DO NOT look at the story on the page below. Fill in the blanks on this page with the words called for. Then, using the words you have selected, fill in the blank spaces in the story.

Now you've created your own hilarious MAD LIBS® game!

# CANAL SURFING

VERB ENDING IN "ING" _____

PLURAL NOUN _____

ADJECTIVE _____

PLURAL NOUN _____

PART OF THE BODY (PLURAL) _____

ADJECTIVE _____

VERB _____

PLURAL NOUN _____

NUMBER _____

COLOR _____

VERB ENDING IN "ING" _____

ADJECTIVE _____

NOUN _____

NOUN _____

NUMBER _____

A PLACE _____

ADVERB _____

PLURAL NOUN _____

# MAD LIBS

# CANAL SURFING

A great underwater earthquake sent a tidal wave _____

_VERB ENDING IN "ING"_

toward Venice, Italy, the city built on _____ floating in the

_PLURAL NOUN_

water. To save the city, its people, and its treasures, Aquaman used his

_____ mental powers to ask the _____ of the sea

_ADJECTIVE_ _PLURAL NOUN_

to help. He commanded the giant squid with their many

_____ to gather _____ boulders from the

_PART OF THE BODY (PLURAL)_ _ADJECTIVE_

bed of the ocean and _____ walls across the mouths

_VERB_

of the city's famous _____ to keep out the floodwaters.

_PLURAL NOUN_

He sent packs of _____-foot-long _____ whales

_NUMBER_ _COLOR_

_____ into the rushing wall of water to slow it down,

_VERB ENDING IN "ING"_

while _____ fish leapt along the city's waterways to warn the

_ADJECTIVE_

citizens of the dangerous approaching _____. Thanks to the

_NOUN_

_____ of the _____ seas, Venice was saved from the

_NOUN_ _NUMBER_

flood. The people of (the) _____ are _____ grateful

_A PLACE_ _ADVERB_

to Aquaman and his finny _____ for all they have done!

_PLURAL NOUN_

From DC COMICS SUPER HERO MAD LIBS® • TM & © DC Comics. (s15).
Published in 2015 by Mad Libs, an imprint of Penguin Random House LLC.

MAD LIBS® is fun to play with friends, but you can also play it by yourself! To begin with, DO NOT look at the story on the page below. Fill in the blanks on this page with the words called for. Then, using the words you have selected, fill in the blank spaces in the story.

Now you've created your own hilarious MAD LIBS® game!

## PUNCH LINE

CITY _____

PLURAL NOUN _____

LAST NAME _____

ADJECTIVE _____

ADJECTIVE _____

VERB _____

VERB _____

NUMBER _____

ADJECTIVE _____

NOUN _____

NOUN _____

NOUN _____

PLURAL NOUN _____

VERB _____

ADJECTIVE _____

FIRST NAME (MALE) _____

# MAD LIBS®
# PUNCH LINE

"The Riddler is back in _____ and he's planning trouble! He
                          CITY

sent us riddles as _____ to his crimes," Commissioner
                        PLURAL NOUN

_____ told Batman. The _____ crime fighter
   LAST NAME                            ADJECTIVE

studied the Riddler's list: *What knows _____ words but will*
                                            ADJECTIVE

*never _____? What will _____ around the world but*
          VERB                      VERB

*always stays in one spot? What starts with a P and ends with an E and has*

*more than _____ letters?* Batman thought for a moment and said,
              NUMBER

"The answers are _____! A dictionary contains every
                     ADJECTIVE

_____ but doesn't speak, a postage _____ stays glued
     NOUN                                        NOUN

to the corner of a/an _____, and the post office has many
                           NOUN

_____!" "That's it! The Riddler's going to _____
   PLURAL NOUN                                              VERB

the post office," Commissioner Gordon cried. But Batman said, "No!

He plans to steal the _____ postage stamp of dictionary writer
                          ADJECTIVE

_____ Webster from the Gotham City Library . . . where
FIRST NAME (MALE)

I'll be waiting for him!"

From DC COMICS SUPER HERO MAD LIBS® • TM & © DC Comics. (s15).
Published in 2015 by Mad Libs, an imprint of Penguin Random House LLC.

MAD LIBS® is fun to play with friends, but you can also play it by yourself! To begin with, DO NOT look at the story on the page below. Fill in the blanks on this page with the words called for. Then, using the words you have selected, fill in the blank spaces in the story.

Now you've created your own hilarious MAD LIBS® game!

# USER FRIENDLY

ADJECTIVE _____

ADJECTIVE _____

COLOR _____

NOUN _____

VERB _____

VERB _____

NOUN _____

PART OF THE BODY (PLURAL) _____

PLURAL NOUN _____

ADVERB _____

NOUN _____

VERB _____

ADVERB _____

ADJECTIVE _____

COLOR _____

PART OF THE BODY _____

NOUN _____

NOUN _____

Doctor Light had cast the city in a/an _____ darkness that left
<u>ADJECTIVE</u>

even the Justice League _____. "Everything has gone
<u>ADJECTIVE</u>

_____!" said Wonder Woman. "Not even my X-ray
<u>COLOR</u>

_____ can see through it!" said Superman. "How can we
<u>NOUN</u>

_____ someone we can't even see?" asked Aquaman. But
<u>VERB</u>

Cyborg said with a/an _____, "The dark's not a/an
<u>VERB</u>

_____ for me! Everybody, put your _____
<u>NOUN</u>                          <u>PART OF THE BODY (PLURAL)</u>

on the shoulder of the person in front of you and follow me!" Cyborg's

fellow _____ did just as he told them, and very soon they
<u>PLURAL NOUN</u>

heard Doctor Light cry out _____, "The Justice
<u>ADVERB</u>

_____! But how did you _____ me when I've turned
<u>NOUN</u>                    <u>VERB</u>

everything _____ dark?" Cyborg stepped forward and grabbed
<u>ADVERB</u>

the _____ villain, crushing the _____-out device
<u>ADJECTIVE</u>                        <u>COLOR</u>

with his robot _____. As the _____ returned,
<u>PART OF THE BODY</u>              <u>NOUN</u>

Cyborg said, "I don't need to explain . . . I'm part _____,
<u>NOUN</u>

complete with built-in radar!"

MAD LIBS® is fun to play with friends, but you can also play it by yourself! To begin with, DO NOT look at the story on the page below. Fill in the blanks on this page with the words called for. Then, using the words you have selected, fill in the blank spaces in the story.

Now you've created your own hilarious MAD LIBS® game!

# FASTER THAN SIGHT

ADJECTIVE _____

ANIMAL _____

PART OF THE BODY (PLURAL) _____

ADJECTIVE _____

NOUN _____

VERB _____

ADJECTIVE _____

NOUN _____

PART OF THE BODY (PLURAL) _____

ADJECTIVE _____

PART OF THE BODY _____

COLOR _____

ADJECTIVE _____

ADVERB _____

NOUN _____

PART OF THE BODY _____

PLURAL NOUN _____

VERB _____

# MAD LIBS®
# FASTER THAN SIGHT

DC COMICS™

"You'll never escape this trap, Flash," Gorilla Grodd, the super-

_____ master of _____ City, growled. "Your
　　ADJECTIVE　　　　　　　　　　　　ANIMAL

_____ are trapped in _____ titanium steel
PART OF THE BODY (PLURAL)　　　　　　　　ADJECTIVE

and you are held by _____ beams that will instantly
　　　　　　　　　　　　NOUN

_____ you if you touch them!" The Flash said, "This certainly
　VERB

is a/an _____ trap, Grodd . . . but it can't hold the Fastest
　　　ADJECTIVE

_____ Alive!" Before Grodd could respond, The Flash
　NOUN

vanished right before his _____! Then the
　　　　　　　　　　　PART OF THE BODY (PLURAL)

_____ villain felt a tap on his _____ and turned to
　ADJECTIVE　　　　　　　　　　　PART OF THE BODY

see the _____ Speedster behind him. "In fact, I'm so
　　　　COLOR

_____, I _____ vibrated between the molecules of
　ADJECTIVE　　　ADVERB

the steel and the laser beams like a/an _____." Then, faster
　　　　　　　　　　　　　　　　　　NOUN

than the _____ could see, The Flash tied up Grodd with wires
　　　　PART OF THE BODY

and _____. "Now, let's see if you can _____ from
　　PLURAL NOUN　　　　　　　　　　　　　VERB

my trap!" The Flash laughed.

MAD LIBS® is fun to play with friends, but you can also play it by yourself! To begin with, DO NOT look at the story on the page below. Fill in the blanks on this page with the words called for. Then, using the words you have selected, fill in the blank spaces in the story.

Now you've created your own hilarious MAD LIBS® game!

# TESTING, TESTING

COLOR _____

NOUN _____

ADJECTIVE _____

ADJECTIVE _____

ADJECTIVE _____

VERB _____

VERB _____

NOUN _____

ADJECTIVE _____

NOUN _____

ADJECTIVE _____

NOUN _____

COLOR _____

NOUN _____

ADJECTIVE _____

VERB _____

ADJECTIVE _____

COLOR _____

Hal Jordan, the alter ego of the super hero _____ Lantern, was
_COLOR_

flying the experimental XK-19 _____ fighter. The
_NOUN_

_____ aircraft zoomed high over the desert. "All systems are
_ADJECTIVE_

_____! I'm going to open her up to _____ speed,"
_ADJECTIVE_ _ADJECTIVE_

Hal reported to the control tower. But once Hal started to accelerate,

he heard an explosion that made the airplane _____ and then
_VERB_

begin to _____ out of control! "Hal! What's wrong?" the
_VERB_

control tower radioed back to him. But Hal couldn't respond . . .

because he was no longer in the _____! The _____
_NOUN_ _ADJECTIVE_

pilot had changed into his Green Lantern _____. Using his
_NOUN_

_____ power _____, he created a giant _____
_ADJECTIVE_ _NOUN_ _COLOR_

ramp from the sky down to the _____. He used his
_NOUN_

_____ powers to guide the XK-19 safely to the ground! "Come
_ADJECTIVE_

in, Hal! Can you _____ me?" the control tower called back.
_VERB_

Hal answered, "I read you loud and _____ . . . I had some
_ADJECTIVE_

_____ warning lights, but they're all green now!"
_COLOR_

MAD LIBS® is fun to play with friends, but you can also play it by yourself! To begin with, DO NOT look at the story on the page below. Fill in the blanks on this page with the words called for. Then, using the words you have selected, fill in the blank spaces in the story.

Now you've created your own hilarious MAD LIBS® game!

# DEEP TROUBLE

PERSON IN ROOM _____

NOUN _____

VERB ENDING IN "ING" _____

NOUN _____

ADJECTIVE _____

A PLACE _____

ADJECTIVE _____

ANIMAL (PLURAL) _____

COLOR _____

PLURAL NOUN _____

VERB _____

ADVERB _____

NOUN _____

PLURAL NOUN _____

A PLACE _____

# MAD LIBS

# DEEP TROUBLE

Hello, my name is _____. As you can see, I'm a dolphin, and
 PERSON IN ROOM

Aquaman is my _____. He knows he can always call me and
 NOUN

I will come _____ as fast as I can. Once, he sent out
 VERB ENDING IN "ING"

a/an _____ call because a group of _____ humans in
 NOUN                              ADJECTIVE

a submarine had come to (the) _____, Aquaman's kingdom
 A PLACE

at the bottom of the sea, to steal its _____ treasures. So
 ADJECTIVE

Aquaman summoned a legion of _____ to squirt globs
 ANIMAL (PLURAL)

of their thick _____ ink all around the submarine so the men
 COLOR

couldn't see. Next, Aquaman called in swordfish and hammerhead

_____ to stab holes through the hull of the ship and
 PLURAL NOUN

_____ on the engine. The submarine was _____
 VERB                                              ADVERB

damaged, but Aquaman would not let the men die, so he asked me and

my fellow dolphins to carry the damaged _____ to the surface
 NOUN

. . . where Aquaman's human _____ took the men away to
 PLURAL NOUN

a place where they could not harm anyone else . . . (the) _____!
 A PLACE

MAD LIBS® is fun to play with friends, but you can also play it by yourself! To begin with, DO NOT look at the story on the page below. Fill in the blanks on this page with the words called for. Then, using the words you have selected, fill in the blank spaces in the story.

Now you've created your own hilarious MAD LIBS® game!

# THE FORTRESS OF SOLITUDE

PLURAL NOUN _____

NOUN _____

NOUN _____

NOUN _____

ADJECTIVE _____

PART OF THE BODY (PLURAL) _____

ADJECTIVE _____

ADJECTIVE _____

SILLY WORD _____

ADJECTIVE _____

NOUN _____

A PLACE _____

COLOR _____

TYPE OF LIQUID _____

LETTER OF THE ALPHABET _____

PART OF THE BODY (PLURAL) _____

A PLACE _____

TYPE OF FOOD _____

Far away from any people or _____ lies Superman's Arctic
PLURAL NOUN

Fortress of _____. Here, the Man of _____ keeps his
NOUN                              NOUN

greatest secrets . . . and weapons from across the _____ that
NOUN

are too _____ to be allowed to fall into the wrong
ADJECTIVE

_____. Today, Superman has brought back a/an
PART OF THE BODY (PLURAL)

_____ new treasure: a/an _____ diamond flower
ADJECTIVE                         ADJECTIVE

from the planet _____. "This will look _____ in my
SILLY WORD                              ADJECTIVE

garden of alien plants, next to the Singing Rock _____ from
NOUN

(the) _____, the _____ Fire Tree of Mercury, and
A PLACE              COLOR

the _____ bush from Dimension _____!
TYPE OF LIQUID              LETTER OF THE ALPHABET

And while I'm here, I'll check to see if the _____
PART OF THE BODY (PLURAL)

Shrub has sprouted any new flowers. I also have to remember to feed

the _____ Crawling Vine . . . It's the only plant in the universe
A PLACE

that eats _____!"
TYPE OF FOOD

MAD LIBS® is fun to play with friends, but you can also play it by yourself! To begin with, DO NOT look at the story on the page below. Fill in the blanks on this page with the words called for. Then, using the words you have selected, fill in the blank spaces in the story.

Now you've created your own hilarious MAD LIBS® game!

# BIG TROUBLE

PERSON IN ROOM _____

NOUN _____

NOUN _____

NUMBER _____

NOUN _____

ADJECTIVE _____

NOUN _____

PART OF THE BODY _____

VERB _____

ADJECTIVE _____

PART OF THE BODY _____

ADJECTIVE _____

COLOR _____

PART OF THE BODY (PLURAL) _____

VERB _____

PLURAL NOUN _____

ADJECTIVE _____

# MAD LIBS®
# BIG TROUBLE

This is _____ in the New York City News traffic helicopter,
　　　　　PERSON IN ROOM

reporting live from the harbor, where the _____ of Liberty is
　　　　　　　　　　　　　　　　　　　　　NOUN

under attack by the giant _____ Giganta! It looks like Giganta
　　　　　　　　　　　　　NOUN

is trying to uproot the _____-foot-tall _____ of freedom
　　　　　　　　　　　NUMBER　　　　　　　　　NOUN

from its base, and police are unable to stop her! Wait a moment . . . It

looks like . . . YES! Here comes Wonder Woman in her amazing

_____ Jet! The Amazon Princess has landed her _____
ADJECTIVE　　　　　　　　　　　　　　　　　　　　　　　　　NOUN

on the statue's _____. Giganta is trying to _____
　　　　　　　PART OF THE BODY　　　　　　　　　　　　　VERB

Wonder Woman away, but the _____ heroine has taken hold
　　　　　　　　　　　　　ADJECTIVE

of the villain's _____ and is using her _____ strength
　　　　　　PART OF THE BODY　　　　　　　　　ADJECTIVE

to flip the giant into the water. Now Wonder Woman is using her

_____ lasso to trap Giganta's _____ and
COLOR　　　　　　　　　　　　　　　　　PART OF THE BODY (PLURAL)

_____ her away. Ladies and _____, the Statue of
VERB　　　　　　　　　　　　　　　　PLURAL NOUN

Liberty is safe, thanks to _____ Woman!
　　　　　　　　　　　　ADJECTIVE

MAD LIBS® is fun to play with friends, but you can also play it by yourself! To begin with, DO NOT look at the story on the page below. Fill in the blanks on this page with the words called for. Then, using the words you have selected, fill in the blank spaces in the story.

Now you've created your own hilarious MAD LIBS® game!

# BRAINPOWER

EXCLAMATION _____

NOUN _____

ADJECTIVE _____

ADJECTIVE _____

COLOR _____

ADVERB _____

ADJECTIVE _____

PLURAL NOUN _____

ADJECTIVE _____

VERB (PAST TENSE) _____

VERB ENDING IN "ING" _____

ADJECTIVE _____

ADJECTIVE _____

ADJECTIVE _____

NOUN _____

ADJECTIVE _____

# MAD LIBS

# BRAINPOWER

"_____!" cried Lex Luthor. "My energy-absorbing robot has
   EXCLAMATION

you trapped, Cyborg, and there's nothing you can do!" Cyborg, the

half-human, half-_____ super hero, was trapped by Luthor's
           NOUN

own _____ robot. Its _____ mechanical eyes gave off
   ADJECTIVE         ADJECTIVE

_____ beams that were _____ draining all the power
   COLOR         ADVERB

from Cyborg. "Soon you'll be too _____ to move, and you'll
         ADJECTIVE

belong to me! I can harness your robotic _____ and use
         PLURAL NOUN

them for my own _____ plans!" Luthor said. Cyborg knew
     ADJECTIVE

that once his power level _____ past a certain point,
       VERB (PAST TENSE)

he would be at Luthor's mercy. But then Cyborg realized that the evil

and deadly robot was _____ up his own power at a/an
     VERB ENDING IN "ING"

_____ and steady rate, and that gave him a/an _____
  ADJECTIVE           ADJECTIVE

idea. "If you want my power this badly, you can take it . . . take it all at

once!" Cyborg cried, and let loose a/an _____ burst of energy.
         ADJECTIVE

The overload of energy was too much for the evil _____, and,
         NOUN

with a loud boom, it collapsed into a/an _____ pile of metal!
         ADJECTIVE

From DC COMICS SUPER HERO MAD LIBS® • TM & © DC Comics. (s15).
Published in 2015 by Mad Libs, an imprint of Penguin Random House LLC.

MAD LIBS® is fun to play with friends, but you can also play it by yourself! To begin with, DO NOT look at the story on the page below. Fill in the blanks on this page with the words called for. Then, using the words you have selected, fill in the blank spaces in the story.

Now you've created your own hilarious MAD LIBS® game!

## THE BATCAVE

OCCUPATION _____

ADJECTIVE _____

PLURAL NOUN _____

NOUN _____

VERB _____

NOUN _____

PLURAL NOUN _____

NOUN _____

ADJECTIVE _____

NOUN _____

VERB _____

ANIMAL _____

ADJECTIVE _____

Sometimes, after he finished cleaning up the Batcave, Batman's

_____, Alfred, liked to pretend he was giving a tour of
<u>OCCUPATION</u>

Batman's _____ headquarters. "Here we have the shelf on
<u>ADJECTIVE</u>

which Batman displays all the _____ he has gathered from
<u>PLURAL NOUN</u>

his many foes, like _____-woman and Mr. _____.
<u>NOUN</u>                                        <u>VERB</u>

This _____ over here once belonged to the Penguin, but
<u>NOUN</u>

instead of using it as protection from the rain, he used it to fire knockout

_____. Next to that is the Joker's playing card, a/an
<u>PLURAL NOUN</u>

_____ that he leaves at every crime scene to remind everyone
<u>NOUN</u>

he is the _____ Prince of Crime. Do not be afraid of this
<u>ADJECTIVE</u>

dinosaur over here . . . It is not real, but rather a mechanical

_____ that Batman once had to _____ on mysterious
<u>NOUN</u>                                       <u>VERB</u>

_____ Island! Thank you for coming, and I hope you enjoyed
<u>ANIMAL</u>

your tour of Batman's _____ lair!"
<u>ADJECTIVE</u>

MAD LIBS® is fun to play with friends, but you can also play it by yourself! To begin with, DO NOT look at the story on the page below. Fill in the blanks on this page with the words called for. Then, using the words you have selected, fill in the blank spaces in the story.

Now you've created your own hilarious MAD LIBS® game!

## A FRIEND IN NEED

COLOR _____

NOUN _____

COLOR _____

ADJECTIVE _____

VERB ENDING IN "ING" _____

ADJECTIVE _____

COLOR _____

PART OF THE BODY _____

NOUN _____

ADJECTIVE _____

PART OF THE BODY _____

COLOR _____

ADJECTIVE _____

BOOM! Sinestro's _____ power ring beam blasted Green
_COLOR_

Lantern into the _____ of a downtown building. Green
_NOUN_

Lantern tried with all his might to fight back, but Sinestro's

_____ power ring was an even match for his own green one.
_COLOR_

"_____ guys never win, Sinestro," Green Lantern growled,
_ADJECTIVE_

but Sinestro didn't listen. He put Green Lantern into the bucket seat of

a gigantic slingshot and sent him _____ across the
_VERB ENDING IN "ING"_

city. But as Sinestro flew into the sky to witness the destruction of his

_____ enemy, he accidentally bumped into a flying man in a
_ADJECTIVE_

blue-and-_____ costume. "Superman!" Sinestro gasped.
_COLOR_

Before he could raise his _____ to use his power ring against
_PART OF THE BODY_

the Man of Steel, Wonder Woman flew in and looped her golden

_____ over him, while The Flash sprinted by at _____
_NOUN_ _ADJECTIVE_

speed and snatched the ring from Sinestro's _____, before
_PART OF THE BODY_

returning carrying the _____ Lantern in his arms! "The
_COLOR_

_____ guys always win, Sinestro . . . with a little help from
_ADJECTIVE_

their friends!"

MAD LIBS® is fun to play with friends, but you can also play it by yourself! To begin with, DO NOT look at the story on the page below. Fill in the blanks on this page with the words called for. Then, using the words you have selected, fill in the blank spaces in the story.

Now you've created your own hilarious MAD LIBS® game!

# A BLACK MANTA DAY FOR ATLANTIS

VERB (PAST TENSE) _____

A PLACE _____

COLOR _____

VERB _____

NOUN _____

COLOR _____

ADJECTIVE _____

PLURAL NOUN _____

NOUN _____

PART OF THE BODY _____

VERB (PAST TENSE) _____

ADVERB _____

NUMBER _____

ADVERB _____

NOUN _____

# MAD LIBS

# A BLACK MANTA DAY
# FOR ATLANTIS

One day, as Aquaman _____ through the undersea
               VERB (PAST TENSE)

kingdom of (the) _____, a/an _____-hot energy
          A PLACE            COLOR

blast exploded the street in front of him. "Do not _____,
                                   VERB

Aquaman . . . or the next _____ will be for you!" called a
                      NOUN

familiar voice from above. Aquaman looked up and saw his enemy

_____ Manta hovering beside his _____ Manta
   COLOR                            ADJECTIVE

ship, which had its _____ aimed at the hero. "I've come
                  PLURAL NOUN

to destroy this city and become the new _____ of Atlantis!"
                                NOUN

Aquaman shook his _____ and said, "There's just one
                PART OF THE BODY

problem with your plan, Manta!" Before Black Manta could

respond, Aquaman _____ himself up at the
                 VERB (PAST TENSE)

invader, swimming too _____ for Manta's weapons to
                   ADVERB

make him their target. Then the hero of the _____ Seas
                            NUMBER

_____ tore the air hoses from Manta's mask, forcing the
  ADVERB

villain to swim to the surface for air. "And the problem is . . . being

_____ of Atlantis is already my job!"
  NOUN

From DC COMICS SUPER HERO MAD LIBS® • TM & © DC Comics. (s15).
Published in 2015 by Mad Libs, an imprint of Penguin Random House LLC.

MAD LIBS® is fun to play with friends, but you can also play it by yourself! To begin with, DO NOT look at the story on the page below. Fill in the blanks on this page with the words called for. Then, using the words you have selected, fill in the blank spaces in the story.

Now you've created your own hilarious MAD LIBS® game!

# SUPERSTAR

ADJECTIVE _____

NOUN _____

ADJECTIVE _____

PART OF THE BODY (PLURAL) _____

PLURAL NOUN _____

NOUN _____

ADJECTIVE _____

COLOR _____

NOUN _____

A PLACE _____

PART OF THE BODY (PLURAL) _____

ADJECTIVE _____

PART OF THE BODY _____

ADVERB _____

NOUN _____

NOUN _____

PLURAL NOUN _____

Starro the Conqueror is one of the Justice League's oldest and most

_____ foes. The giant _____ from another world has
   ADJECTIVE                       NOUN

used his _____ powers to do evil deeds, like control human
            ADJECTIVE

_____ , and launch nuclear _____ at
PART OF THE BODY (PLURAL)                  PLURAL NOUN

Earth's great cities. Now, Starro is at it again, but the _____
                                                           NOUN

League is there to put a stop to his _____ plan. As The Flash,
                                 ADJECTIVE

Wonder Woman, _____ Lantern, and Cyborg battle the alien
                    COLOR

_____ , Superman flies to the missile base located in (the)
   NOUN

_____ . "Don't let Starro into your head," The Flash warns his
   A PLACE

friends. "And shield your _____ !" Cyborg cries
                           PART OF THE BODY (PLURAL)

before shooting a laser that causes a/an _____ burst of light
                                      ADJECTIVE

that blinds Starro's _____ . Then, while the creature is
                     PART OF THE BODY

_____ blind, Green Lantern makes a/an _____ with
   ADVERB                                       NOUN

his power ring to trap Starro and fling him far away into outer space.

At the same time, Superman arrives at the _____ base a split
                                       NOUN

second before the brainwashed general can launch his _____
                                                  PLURAL NOUN

and uses his X-ray vision to melt the controls!

MAD LIBS® is fun to play with friends, but you can also play it by yourself! To begin with, DO NOT look at the story on the page below. Fill in the blanks on this page with the words called for. Then, using the words you have selected, fill in the blank spaces in the story.

Now you've created your own hilarious MAD LIBS® game!

## SUPER HERO HELP WANTED

ADJECTIVE _____

NOUN _____

NOUN _____

VERB _____

ADJECTIVE _____

NOUN _____

FIRST NAME (MALE) _____

EXCLAMATION _____

ADJECTIVE _____

PERSON IN ROOM (MALE) _____

NOUN _____

ADVERB _____

PART OF THE BODY _____

NUMBER _____

# MAD LIBS®

## SUPER HERO
## HELP WANTED

**DC COMICS™**

In the help-wanted section of the _____ *Planet*, Cyborg saw

                ADJECTIVE

an ad for a super hero. "_____ *Wanted*," the ad read. *"Must be*

            NOUN

*stronger than the school bully, run as fast as a track* _____, *and*

                  NOUN

*it would be good if he could also* _____. *He can't be afraid of any*

            VERB

*kid, not even the ones that are a lot more* _____ *than him. He*

              ADJECTIVE

*doesn't have to wear a/an* _____ *like Superman or Batman, but*

            NOUN

*it would be cool if he did. Please reply to* _____." Cyborg

             FIRST NAME (MALE)

thought, *I'd better respond to this ad myself!* Later, Cyborg met the boy

who had placed the ad, who said, "_____! I never expected

           EXCLAMATION

a/an _____ hero would actually answer me! When that bully

  ADJECTIVE

_____ sees that you're my _____, I'll bet he

PERSON IN ROOM (MALE)          NOUN

stops picking on me right away!" Cyborg _____ held up his

           ADVERB

_____ and gave the boy a high _____.

PART OF THE BODY         NUMBER

From DC COMICS SUPER HERO MAD LIBS® • TM & © DC Comics. (s15).
Published in 2015 by Mad Libs, an imprint of Penguin Random House LLC.

MAD LIBS® is fun to play with friends, but you can also play it by yourself! To begin with, DO NOT look at the story on the page below. Fill in the blanks on this page with the words called for. Then, using the words you have selected, fill in the blank spaces in the story.

Now you've created your own hilarious MAD LIBS® game!

# PARADISE

NOUN _____

NOUN _____

NOUN _____

ADJECTIVE _____

ANIMAL (PLURAL) _____

ADJECTIVE _____

PLURAL NOUN _____

NOUN _____

ADJECTIVE _____

PLURAL NOUN _____

ANIMAL _____

ADJECTIVE _____

NOUN _____

PLURAL NOUN _____

# MAD LIBS

# PARADISE

On Paradise _____, home of the warrior women known as
_____NOUN_____

the Amazons, Queen Hippolyta remembered what it was like when her

daughter Diana was still a/an _____, before she became
_____NOUN

Wonder Woman. "Even as a/an _____, Diana wasn't like any
_____NOUN

other child. She was always going off on _____ adventures all
_____ADJECTIVE

over the island, chasing _____ through the forest, hiking
_____ANIMAL (PLURAL)

the _____ hills, or challenging the other _____ to
____ADJECTIVE_____PLURAL NOUN

contests of strength and speed. Why, she was using a bow and

_____ to hunt while her _____ friends were still
____NOUN_____ADJECTIVE

playing with _____! And when her pet _____ was
_____PLURAL NOUN_____ANIMAL

lost in the _____ Cavern of _____, Diana raced
_____ADJECTIVE_____NOUN

right in to save the poor thing. Yes, I suppose I knew from the very start

that my daughter was destined to grow up to become one of the world's

greatest _____."
_____PLURAL NOUN

MAD LIBS® is fun to play with friends, but you can also play it by yourself! To begin with, DO NOT look at the story on the page below. Fill in the blanks on this page with the words called for. Then, using the words you have selected, fill in the blank spaces in the story.

Now you've created your own hilarious MAD LIBS® game!

# DANGER ZONE

OCCUPATION _____

ADJECTIVE _____

PLURAL NOUN _____

ADJECTIVE _____

VERB ENDING IN "ING" _____

PART OF THE BODY (PLURAL) _____

NOUN _____

PLURAL NOUN _____

ADJECTIVE _____

ARTICLE OF CLOTHING _____

NOUN _____

# MAD LIBS

# DANGER ZONE

The citizens of Metropolis had to run for their lives when the escaped

Phantom Zone _____ Jax-Ur came to Earth to use his
                OCCUPATION

_____ powers to smash _____ and destroy
ADJECTIVE                        PLURAL NOUN

buildings. "Ha-ha! I am from the planet Krypton, and I have the same

_____ powers as Superman. But he's off _____
ADJECTIVE                                          VERB ENDING IN "ING"

in outer space, so there's no one on Earth to stop me!" Then Jax-Ur

turned his glowing _____ on the Daily Planet
                     PART OF THE BODY (PLURAL)

Building and said, "Let's see what happens when I use my _____
                                                            NOUN

vision on Superman's best _____!" But before Jax-Ur could
                            PLURAL NOUN

destroy the building, Superman appeared in front of him and pulled

a/an _____ device from under his _____.
      ADJECTIVE                              ARTICLE OF CLOTHING

He used the device to make Jax-Ur surrender and saved the city! "Sorry

it took me so long to get here, but I had to make a quick stop at the

Fortress of _____ to pick up the Phantom Zone Projector. I
              NOUN

need it to send Jax-Ur back where he belongs!"

From DC COMICS SUPER HERO MAD LIBS® • TM & © DC Comics. (s15).
Published in 2015 by Mad Libs, an imprint of Penguin Random House LLC.

MAD LIBS® is fun to play with friends, but you can also play it by yourself! To begin with, DO NOT look at the story on the page below. Fill in the blanks on this page with the words called for. Then, using the words you have selected, fill in the blank spaces in the story.

Now you've created your own hilarious MAD LIBS® game!

# A DARK NIGHT WITH THE DARK KNIGHT

ADJECTIVE _____

PLURAL NOUN _____

VERB ENDING IN "ING" _____

NOUN _____

NOUN _____

PERSON IN ROOM _____

OCCUPATION (PLURAL) _____

ADJECTIVE _____

CELEBRITY _____

VEHICLE _____

ADJECTIVE _____

A PLACE _____

ADJECTIVE _____

Dear Diary,

I have just returned from another _____ night patrolling the
                                   ADJECTIVE

_____ of Gotham City. The sun had barely set before I
PLURAL NOUN

stopped two criminals from _____ a bank. No sooner
                            VERB ENDING IN "ING"

was that done than a/an _____ alarm went off. Someone was
                         NOUN

trying to rob the home of the famous _____ collector,
                                      NOUN

_____. After I handed the evil criminal over to the
PERSON IN ROOM

_____, I drove the Batmobile to Arkham Asylum to see
OCCUPATION (PLURAL)

if any of my most _____ foes, like _____, had
                   ADJECTIVE                CELEBRITY

escaped. On my way there, a call came over the police radio that they

needed help to catch a/an _____ packed with _____
                          VEHICLE                    ADJECTIVE

jewel thieves. Finally, as the sun rose high over the city, I returned to

(the) _____, satisfied that once more I had been able to
      A PLACE

protect the people of my _____ city.
                          ADJECTIVE

**Download Mad Libs today!**

Join the millions of Mad Libs fans
creating wacky and wonderful
stories on our apps!